Valuers' Briefing

Valuations for Financial Reporting under IFRS

Real estate and other tangible assets

Chris Thorne FRICS

Valuology

Important Notice

This Valuers' Briefing has been prepared by an experienced professional valuer based on information available on the date of publication. It is the reader's responsibility to establish that the information is current and correct before relying upon it. Any advice or opinions provided represent the views of the author, and alternative views may exist. No responsibility for loss or damage caused to any person acting or refraining from action as a result of the material included in this publication can be accepted by Valuology Ltd or the author.

Copyright in all or part of this publication is the property of Valuology Ltd. Save where and to the extent expressly permitted within this document, no part of this work may be reproduced or used in any form or by any means including graphic, electronic, or mechanical, including photocopying, recording, taping or web distribution, without the written permission of Valuology Ltd. See www.valuology.org

© Valuology 2019

ISBN: 9781655106361

Preface

Valuation professionals are often called upon to provide valuations for a company or other organisation for use in the preparation of its accounts. However, unless the valuer has an accounting background some of the terminology associated with accounting, and in particular the preparation of financial statements can be mystifying. Another problem is that some words and phrases are common to both accounting and valuation practice but can have quite different meanings in the different contexts. This can lead to misunderstanding between valuers and their clients.

Some requests may seem strange to a valuer as they involve hypotheses that would not be encountered in the real world. For example, why would a valuer be asked to value the land on which a building stands separately from that building, when the two could only be bought or sold together? What is meant by an "impairment test" on a machine that is functioning perfectly well? Why would a valuer place separate values on the engines of a plane from the rest of the aircraft? Why does a building need to be valued without its air conditioning?

This briefing is written by a valuer for valuers to help them unravel some of these mysteries. It explains the accounting concepts used in preparing financial statements that commonly require valuation inputs and how these valuations will be used in an organisation's accounts. This should help the valuer understand the most appropriate approach and assumptions for preparing the valuation.

Valuations may be required for most types of asset or liability owned or held by an organisation. The focus of this briefing is on the valuation of tangible assets, such as real estate, plant and machinery. Some of the accounting standards discussed also apply to financial instruments, such as shares, options and derivatives, or to intangible assets such as intellectual property, customer lists, trademarks or copyright. Some of these have dedicated accounting standards of their own. While in some organisations the value of such financial and intangible assets can considerably outweigh the tangible assets, they are outside the scope of this briefing because it is very rare for a valuer with expertise in valuing tangible assets to also deal with non-tangibles.

The accounting standards discussed are exclusively the International Financial Reporting Standards (IFRSs) as issued by the IASB. These are the most widely used accounting standards globally, especially for larger organisations and those that are listed on public exchanges. There are also many nationally based standards in use which contain similar concepts to those in the IFRSs, although the detail may differ.

The objective of the discussion of various IFRSs is to help a professional valuer understand the valuation requirement and the key criteria that apply. It is written for valuers, not accounting professionals, and is not intended to be a comprehensive guide to any of the financial reporting standards mentioned. All the standards referenced are subject to review by the IASB and whilst the summary of the elements relevant to valuation is correct at the time of publication, a valuer undertaking this work should always check whether the relevant standards have been subsequently amended.

Contents

Chapter 1	Introduction	1
	What are Financial Statements?	1
	Financial Reporting Standards around the world	2
	International Financial Reporting Standards (IFRS)	3
Chapter 2	IFRS 13 - Fair Value Measurements	7
	Fair Value Definition	7
	The Unit of Account	9
	Highest and Best Use	10
	Methods	13
	Inputs	14
	Disclosures	16
Chapter 3	IAS 2: Inventories	17
Chapter 4	IAS 16: Property, plant and equipment	19
	Depreciation	21
Chapter 5	IAS 36: Impairment of assets	25
	Value in use	26
Chapter 6	IAS 40: Investment property	27
	Fair value model	27
	Cost Model	28
	Investment property under construction	29
Chapter 7	IAS 41: Agriculture	31
Chapter 8	IFRS 3: Business combinations	35
Chapter 9	IFRS 5: Non-current assets held for sale and discontinued operations	37
Chapter 10	IFRS 16: Leases	39
	Lessees	39
	Lessors	42
Chapter 11	Professional Requirements	47
Illustrative Examples		51
IE 1	An owner occupied property with a limited market	51
IE2	Calculating the depreciable amount of a building	55
About the Author		59

Chapter 1 Introduction

This chapter provides an overview of the purpose of financial statements and of some of the standards that can apply to their preparation, highlighting those where valuation inputs may be required.

There is nothing fundamentally different about how valuations required for preparing a financial statement are carried out. The valuer still needs to make the usual investigations and enquiries and will use one or more of the commonly recognised valuation methods. However, the relevant financial reporting standards, also known as accounting standards, can set specific criteria for what may be valued, the assumptions that are appropriate and what needs to be disclosed about the valuation. A basic understanding of the relevant standard and the context in which the valuation is required is therefore important for any valuer providing valuations for this purpose.

What are Financial Statements?

Financial statements, sometimes also known as financial reports, are produced by an entity (i.e. any incorporated or unincorporated body or organisation) to provide information about its financial position, performance and changes in its financial position that is useful to management, owners and other stakeholders in making economic decisions. A complete set of financial statements will typically include:

- A balance sheet, also referred to as a

"statement of financial position", which provides a statement of the entity's assets, liabilities, and owners' equity at a given point in time.

- An income statement, also known as a "statement of comprehensive income", or "profit and loss account", which reports on an entity's income, expenses, and profits over a given period of time.
- An equity statement or statement of retained earnings, which reports on the changes in equity of the entity during the stated period.
- A cash flow statement which on an entity's cash flow activities, particularly its operating, investing and financing activities.

The term "financial statement" specifically relates to accounting information published for the benefit of the public or investors, whereas the word "accounts" is a generic term that can include other types of document, for example, management accounts for internal use only.

Financial Reporting Standards around the world

The most widely used standards used for compiling financial statements are the International Financial Reporting Standards (IFRS), issued by the International Accounting Standards Board (IASB). However, although the most ubiquitous set of standards, not all countries use them, and even in those that do, they often are not required for non-listed companies or smaller entities.

While there is now considerable global convergence in the financial reporting standards used in the private sector, particularly for companies listed on a public stock exchange, there remains considerable diversity in the public sector. Most governments have regulations relating to the preparation of public sector accounts within their jurisdiction, but there is considerable diversity between them. Although there is a set of International Public Sector Accounting Standards (IPSAS) these are not widely adopted. Some of the greatest diversity between different jurisdictions is around which public assets should be measured in financial statements and how they should be measured. Where assets are required to be valued there is often prescription as to how those valuations are calculated, and some of the methods prescribed by some jurisdictions differ from normal market practice.

It will therefore be appreciated that it is of fundamental importance that the valuer establishes which accounting standards or other regulations are applicable before undertaking a valuation for inclusion in a financial statement.

International Financial Reporting Standards (IFRS)

There are currently 144 countries that require the use of the IFRSs for all or most publicly accountable entities, including all those in the European Union. Of the G20, the twenty largest world economies, fifteen require the use of IFRS. Of the five that do not, China, India and Indonesia have developed domestic standards that are in line with IFRS, Japan allows voluntary adoption of IFRS and the USA allows foreign based entities to use IFRS for filings in the USA, as well as having followed a path to converge many of the US standards with the equivalent under IFRS.

The IFRSs encompass a conceptual framework for the preparation and presentation of financial statements together with individual standards on different topics and supporting interpretations. In 2019, there are forty five individual standards. Standards originally published before 2001 have the prefix IAS and those published since are prefixed IFRS.

Many of the individual standards permit or require valuation and one, IFRS 13 Fair Value Measurements, sets the criteria for valuation in most of the other standards. Besides IFRS 13, the standards most likely to be encountered by a valuer of tangible assets are:

IAS 2   -   Inventories

IAS 16   -   Property, plant and equipment

IAS 36   -   Impairment of assets

IAS 40   -   Investment property

IAS 41   -   Agriculture

IFRS 3   -   Business combinations

IFRS 5 -   Non-current assets held for sale and discontinued operations

IFRS 16 -   Leases

Because the focus of this briefing is mainly on tangible assets, those standards that deal exclusively with financial instruments or intangible assets are not referenced, although it should be appreciated that many of the valuation requirements discussed apply to these items as well.

While a valuer does not need an in depth knowledge of each of the above standards, an appreciation of the basic accounting objective of each is necessary to ensure that appropriate advice is provided. The following chapters provide a synopsis of the valuation provisions contained in each of the above mentioned standards.

Chapter 2 IFRS 13 - Fair Value Measurements

For many years, various IFRS standards required or permitted assets and liabilities to be measured at "fair value" but difficulties arose because there was not a common understanding of what was meant by fair value, nor of the assumptions that should apply when estimating it in different situations. Impetus for the development of a standard for fair value was also provided by a 2006 agreement between the IASB and the USA standard setter, the FASB, to develop common requirements for its measurement and for the appropriate disclosures that should be made. As a result, IFRS 13 *Fair Value Measurements*, which was published in 2011 and effective from 2013, is almost identical to its equivalent under US Generally Accepted Accounting Principles (US GAAP), known as "Topic 820".

Fair Value Definition

Fair Value is defined in IFRS 13 as: *"...the price that would be received to sell an asset or paid to transfer a liability in an orderly transaction between market participants at the measurement date."* ©IFRS Foundation

The standard provides considerable guidance on how the elements of this concise definition are to be interpreted and applied, for example with discussion on the market in which the transaction is deemed to take place, the nature and motivation of the parties to the transaction, what represents the most advantageous price, how the principle of highest and best use applies, to name but a few.

Many real property valuers will be more familiar with Market Value, as defined in the International Valuation Standards (IVS) than with Fair Value as defined above. However, for most practical purposes the two should produce the same result as they are both based on the same concept of a price in a free and open exchange between typical buyers and sellers on a given date. It follows that both reflect the principle of highest and best use, which follows logically from the presumption that the parties are informed, acting in their best interests and acting without constraint. The very few cases where Fair Value arguably may differ from Market Value arise in situations which are unlikely to be encountered when valuing tangible assets and are therefore not discussed in this briefing.

IFRS 13 describes Fair Value as an "exit price". Some commentators cite this as difference from the IVS Market Value, as the latter does not use the term in either the definition or the extended conceptual framework that accompanies it in IVS 104. However, this is a distinction without a difference. Both definitions include a hypothetical transaction and in that transaction the buying party is "entering" and the selling party is "exiting". The agreed price is therefore an entry price for the buyer and an exit price for the seller. Its use in IFRS 13 is to emphasise that the reporting entity is deemed to be selling the asset in the market that exists on the reporting date. This means that whether the entity has any actual intention to sell, whether it would be willing to sell at the Fair Value or whether it has a strategic reason which would make it willing to pay more to acquire the asset in question are all irrelevant to the Fair Value measurement. None of this differs from the Market Value hypothesis.

The good news is that a valuer who understands Market Value and applies its concepts and principles correctly will in virtually all cases be providing a value consistent with IFRS Fair Value. In the writer's experience this is recognised and accepted by most auditors of financial statements, so it is not essential for the valuer undertaking the occasional financial statement valuation to make a detailed study of IFRS 13. However, a few of the key issues that are addressed in IFRS 13 are now highlighted.

The Unit of Account

IFRS 13 provides that the asset or liability to be valued may be either a standalone item or a group of items. Which is appropriate depends on the "unit of account", and this is generally determined by the accounting standard that permits or requires the Fair Value to be determined. Understanding the unit of account is therefore an essential prerequisite for any valuation prepared for financial reporting as it defines what is to be included or excluded.

Unfortunately, the expression "unit of account" to describe what is to be valued separately is not always used in other IFRS standards to define what is to be valued. For example, IAS 16, *Property Plant and Equipment* uses the term "Unit of Measure" , and goes on to explain that this is not defined but is a matter for judgement, although it also indicates that it may be appropriate to aggregate individually insignificant items, such as moulds, tools and dies, associated with a particular machine in a single value. Likewise, IAS 40 *Investment Property* indicates that judgement is sometimes required to determine whether the acquisition of investment property is the acquisition of an asset or a group of assets, or even a business combination falling under IFRS 3.

In practice, the valuer will normally be able to recognise what is the appropriate unit of account based on their knowledge of the appropriate market. Unless stipulated otherwise, for example in the depreciation provisions under IAS 16, this will be how notionally separable items are normally aggregated in a transaction to maximise marketability and price. However, if in doubt this needs to be discussed and agreed with the client or other advisors responsible for the preparation of the financial statements.

Highest and Best Use

A problem that has vexed valuers for many years is whether the asset is to be valued as part of the business or as a standalone asset. A common example of the dilemma is where an industrial process is situated on land which would have potential for a more valuable use if sold separately due to changes in the locality and market since the industrial process was established. In terms of reporting an entity's financial performance, it clearly would be illogical and misleading to measure interdependent assets on different assumptions, i.e. the land on the basis of the value it could achieve if sold for a different purpose but the buildings, process plant and equipment on the basis that they would remain operating in situ.

IFRS 13 deals with this conundrum by stipulating that if the highest and best use of the asset is to use it in combination with other assets, the Fair Value of the asset is the price that would be received to sell the asset assuming that the asset would be used with those other assets and that those assets would be available to the buyer. In contrast, if a buyer would pay the highest price for the asset on a standalone basis, that is the Fair Value of the asset.

The situation is therefore not as simple as disregarding a higher value for an alternative use of the land providing management intend to continue the existing operations at that location. A comparison needs to be made between:

- the value of the land for industrial use. This would assume that all assets currently used in combination with the land were present, although these may be separately valued or measured in the financial statements. This could include items such as the buildings any fixed process plant and equipment. Services and infrastructure to the land may also need to be reflected if not reflected elsewhere.

- the value of the land as a vacant site for an alternative use, taking into account the costs of demolishing the existing buildings, removing plant and equipment, decontamination and other decommissioning costs. Any costs, including those arising from delay or uncertainty in achieving the alternative use will also need to be reflected.

Under IFRS 13 the higher of these two figures represents the Fair Value for reporting purposes.

It can be seen that a significant amount of work is potentially required to establish whether the highest and best use is in combination with other assets utilised in the business or for an alternative use. In practice, a valuer is only likely to be called upon to make a detailed analysis in cases where the values are high in relation to the overall business of the reporting entity and the highest and best use not obvious from an initial simple observation of the key criteria.

It is more likely that the valuer of the tangible assets may be commissioned to provide the value on one or other of the above scenarios, perhaps on a specific set of assumptions, in order to assist the reporting entity in establishing the correct Fair Value for reporting purposes, as inputs into this decision may be being provided by other experts. As with all valuation assignments, precisely identifying what is to be valued, the necessary assumptions and clarifying the limits which apply to the investigations is essential.

Methods

IFRS 13 requires the Fair Value to be measured using valuation "techniques" that are appropriate in the circumstances and for which sufficient data is available. The standard indicates that the most widely used techniques used to estimate Fair Value are the market approach, income approach and cost approach, but does not require any one to be used in any given situation, and also indicates that in some cases the use of more than one valuation technique may be appropriate.

Although "valuation methods" is the term more commonly used by professional valuers, the use of "valuation techniques" can be regarded as having the same meaning. In 2016 the FASB in the USA made a small amendment to Topic 820 Fair Value Measurements (its equivalent of IFRS 13) to clarify that within each of the three main valuation "approaches" there were multiple "techniques" with the examples provided of techniques confirming that these are synonymous with "methods". Given that IFRS 13 and Topic 820 are converged standards, the IASB will have been consulted over this change and no significance should be attached to any perceived difference between "methods" and "techniques".

It follows that any method, or combination of methods,

used to estimate Market Value can also be used to estimate Fair Value.

Inputs

IFRS 13 requires the use of relevant "observable" inputs to be maximised and the use of "unobservable" inputs to be minimised. An observable input is one that uses market data sourced from actual events or transactions, whereas an unobservable input is one that is not based on market data but is a best estimate based on the assumptions that market participants would make when pricing the asset.

Once again, although the terminology may be unfamiliar, the principle should be familiar to any professional valuer; you give most weight to data from the relevant market but where this is scarce or not available you have to use your professional judgement to estimate how a prospective buyer or seller would price the asset.

Another important concept to understand is the input hierarchy in IFRS 13. The standard defines and categorises the inputs used in the valuation into three levels:

- Level 1 Inputs are quoted prices in active markets for identical assets.
- Level 2 Inputs are any inputs other than a quoted price for an identical asset which are indirectly or indirectly observable. Examples include quoted prices for similar assets in an

active market or for identical assets in an inactive market.
- Level 3 inputs are all unobservable inputs, see explanation above.

The hierarchy is designed not to rank the reliability of the valuations but as a means of managing the disclosures that need to be made about the Fair Value in the financial statements. An entity is required to make different disclosures depending on the input level used or when there is a change in the level between successive statements.

From a practical perspective, the valuer may be asked to provide information about the inputs used in arriving at the valuation, and possibly to even pass an opinion on which level is appropriate, although the decision on the latter is a matter for the entity and the advisers directly concerned with the preparation of the statements. If Level 1 inputs are available it is unlikely that a valuer will be involved as no valuation techniques or expertise is required, the current price can be just looked up. A few very liquid types of fixed asset may have inputs that meet the Level 2 criteria, but the general consensus is that most real property valuations will be in Level 3. Property markets are relatively illiquid and the fact that no two properties are strictly identical means that even where good price data is available, some "unobservable" adjustments will be required to reflect differences in design, size, quality, location, etc. Accordingly, the need for estimates based on judgements about how market participants would price the property tends to be the rule rather than the exception when valuing real property interests.

Disclosures

The reporting entity is required to make certain disclosures about Fair Value measurements used in its financial statements. These are the responsibility of the reporting entity, but the valuer should be prepared to provide sufficient information about the inputs and methods used in estimating the value to enable these disclosures to be made. In particular, if there has been a change in the valuation technique used since the last reported value, the entity must not only disclose the change but provide the reasons for it, and this is something that the valuer will need to disclose when reporting.

IFRS 13 provides the foundation for how Fair Value is to be estimated. Other IFRS standards determine what is valued, when the value is required and how the value is to be used. Each of the following Chapters provides a synopsis of the valuation provisions in standards that are most likely to be relevant to the valuer of fixed assets.

Chapter 3 IAS 2: Inventories

In accounting parlance "Inventories" are assets held for sale in the ordinary course of business, which includes finished goods, work-in-process, raw materials and supplies to be used in the production process or in the provision of services.

Inventories can include land and buildings held for sale, e.g. a stock of unsold houses held by a property developer. IAS 2 excludes construction works in progress, financial instruments, biological assets used in agricultural activity and agricultural produce at the point of harvest, all of which are the subject of other IFRSs.

Inventories are measured at the lower of cost or "net realisable value", which is "the estimated selling price in the ordinary course of business less the estimated costs of completion and the estimated costs necessary to make the sale. The standard makes a distinction between net realisable value and Fair Value, indicating that the former is specific to the entity and the latter the price that could be obtained in the market.

For some types of business or asset, e.g. the stock of a retailer, the distinction made between net realisable value and Fair Value less costs to sell is pertinent because the amount realised will vary significantly depending upon the chosen method of disposal, and whether this is to a trade buyer or retail customers. However, in the case of land and buildings held for sale by a builder or developer there is unlikely to be a material difference as the price obtainable on a sale in the normal course of business will normally be the Market Value of each property. An exception would be if the developer's business model was to build in bulk with the intention of selling to an institutional investor or public sector body who would let or sell the individual units, see also the comments on the "Unit of Account" in IFRS 13.

The key issue that differentiates a valuation of inventory under IFRS 5 is that the valuer needs to understand the owning entity's business model and disposal strategy in order to advise on the net realisable value and ignore alternatives that might result in a different realisation.

Chapter 4 IAS 16: Property, plant and equipment

This standard applies to property, plant and equipment (PP&E) expected to be used for more than one accounting period and used in the production or supply of goods and services, for administration or for rental to others. It excludes investment property. And although "plant" in the heading means equipment used in the production of goods or services, under an amendment made in 2014 it now applies to certain biological plants as well. These are so called "bearer plants", i.e. a living plant expected to bear produce for more than one reporting period. However, IAS 16 does not apply to other agricultural assets.

When an item of PP&E is first recognised, i.e. included in an entity's financial statement, it is measured at cost. In subsequent periods it may be measured at either cost less depreciation and accumulated impairment (the "cost model") or at Fair Value less subsequent depreciation and accumulated impairment (the "revaluation model"). Under the revaluation model the Fair Value is determined according to IFRS 13.

Valuations might therefore be required if the entity has opted for the revaluation model. There is no fixed period between revaluations, but IAS 16 requires a revaluation whenever the Fair Value of a revalued asset differs materially from its carrying amount, i.e. the amount currently appearing in the financial statements. In practice, an entity may need to commission a valuation to establish if the current Fair Value differs materially from the carrying amount, even if the new valuation is not then carried forward into the financial statements.

The standard also stipulates that if one item of PP&E is revalued, all other items of the same class or type must also be revalued, in order to prevent selective revaluation of some items and not others.

In practice, only a minority of entities opt for the revaluation model. For most plant and equipment, the economic life is limited and the asset worth relatively little at the end of that period. Systematic depreciation of the initial cost over that period is unlikely to vary significantly from the Fair Value on any given date. In contrast, real property can have an enduring value and can appreciate over time, with the result that the current value can far exceed the initial cost less depreciation. However, while regular revaluations of an entity's property holdings might strengthen its balance sheet and give a better reflection of its overall financial position, the advantage of this is often offset by the need to make increased annual depreciation charges against profit.

While the revaluation model is not as widely used as the cost model to establish the amount attributed to the asset on an entity's balance sheet, i.e. the "carrying amount", valuation advice is often required in order to assist implementation of the depreciation provisions in

IAS 16, which are now discussed.

Depreciation

Depreciation in the context of financial reporting is an expense charged against income to reflect the consumption of an asset over its useful life to the entity. This expense is an apportionment of the "depreciable amount", which is the difference between the carrying amount (determined by either the cost model or the revaluation model described above) and the "residual amount", which is any value remaining at the end of the asset's useful life to the entity.

An entity has discretion over the apportionment of the depreciable amount applied to each period as long as it reflects the pattern at which the benefits of the asset are consumed over its useful life. Depreciation in this context should not be confused with the way the word is used in valuation, for example when applying the depreciated replacement cost (DRC) method. The Fair Value of an asset can be determined using the DRC method under the revaluation model and then the entity will need to decide on the appropriate depreciation charge to apply to this Fair Value as a separate exercise.

Another point that valuers need to note is that the depreciation charge is over the useful life to the entity. This means it is an entity specific measure, which may differ from the useful life as viewed by another market participant. For example, a valuer may judge a building as typically having a remaining economic life of at least twenty years, but if it houses a business operation which the entity estimates will cease within five years, the useful life to the entity is the shorter period.

The residual value and useful life to the entity should be reviewed at least at every financial year end, and the depreciation charge adjusted accordingly. The residual value is the amount that the entity could currently obtain from disposal of an asset, after deducting the costs of disposal, if the asset were already of the age and in the condition expected at the end of its useful life.

IAS 16 requires separate depreciation of any component of an asset that has a cost that is significant in relation to the whole and which may have different useful lives. The standard gives the example of an aircraft, where the engines may be depreciated separately from the airframe. Components that have a similar useful life and that are depreciated in a similar manner may be grouped.

The standard regards land and buildings as separable assets, even if they are acquired together. This means that valuers are frequently asked to provide either a value of the land component alone or an apportionment of the value of the whole between the land and the buildings. The land is not normally depreciated, except in special cases such as quarry or landfill sites.

An apportionment of the current value of the whole property is normally done by deducting the value of the land element in order to establish the proportion that can be attributed to the building(s). It is important to note that the proportion of the overall value thus established is not necessarily the same as the depreciable amount of the building if the useful life to the entity of the building is less than the economic life that is reflected in the value of the whole property. Where this is the case, the valuer will also need to estimate the residual value of the building. This is its value on the reporting date but assuming that it is of the age and in the condition expected at the end of its useful life to the entity.

Confusion sometimes arises as to the basis on which land on which buildings have been constructed should be valued. Is the value confined to the existing use or is it the value that could be obtained assuming that the buildings were at the end of their useful life at the date of valuation? IAS 16 provides that an increase in the value of the land on which a building stands does not affect the determination of the depreciable amount of the building. Accordingly, for the purpose of calculating the depreciable amount attributable to the buildings, the land value for the existing use of the buildings should be used. If the value of the land is higher for an alternative use, this should also be reported, as it could be material to the entity's view of the useful life of the buildings.

A worked example showing the calculation of the

depreciable amount of a building is included as IE 2 in the Illustrative Examples at the end of this briefing.

While IAS16 has a specific requirement to treat land and buildings as separable assets, with depreciation only normally appropriate for the latter, the general rule that any component of an asset that a) has a cost which is significant in relation to the whole, and b) has a significantly different useful life, may mean that the valuer is requested to apportion the value of a building between its components.

A typical request is to allocate values between the fabric of the building and its services for heating, cooling, ventilation etc, as the services can often account for a significant proportion of the overall cost of a building but will typically have a shorter life expectancy than the structure.

IAS 16 does not prescribe how values should be allocated between components of an asset, and the valuer has an obvious difficulty where it clearly would be impractical, if not impossible to sell a component which is an integral part of the overall asset, for example the service installations in a building. However, in the writer's experience, providing a clear rationale is provided, for example looking at the proportion of the overall building cost that is attributable to its services and applying a similar apportionment to the current Fair Value of the whole building, objections are unlikely to be raised by the auditors of the entity's accounts.

Chapter 5 IAS 36: Impairment of assets

Impairment is the term applied in accounting theory when the carrying amount of an asset exceeds the amount that can be recovered from either its use or sale. IAS 36 requires entities to review assets each reporting date for any indication of impairment. Impairment might be indicated by a reduction in the value because of market or technological changes, obsolescence, underperformance in comparison to the expected return or an intention to discontinue or restructure operations.

If impairment has arisen, the carrying amount of the asset, whether derived from either historic cost or a previous valuation, should be written down to the "recoverable amount". This the higher of the asset's Fair Value less costs of disposal or its "value in use." Fair value is determined in accordance with IFRS 13, and disposal costs are those directly attributable to the disposal, excluding finance and any tax liability arising on disposal. The calculation of value in use is discussed below.

If the recoverable amount of an individual asset cannot be easily determined, e.g. because it is inseparable from other complementary assets, it should be determined for the smallest group of assets to which the asset belongs which generates independent cash flows, known as a "cash-generating unit". Examples could include different machines that have been integrated into a production line or land with specialised buildings and equipment that are interdependent in the production of a product or service.

Value in use

Value in use is defined as the present value of the future cash flows expected to be derived from the asset or cash-generating unit. Value in use is specific to the entity as it reflects the cash flows that the entity expects to obtain from continuing use of an asset over its anticipated useful life, including any proceeds from its ultimate disposal. The standard sets criteria for matters that should be reflected in this discounted cash flow analysis, and any valuer instructed to calculate value in use should familiarise themselves with these. In summary, the estimated cash flows have to be reasonable having regard to previous actual outcomes and then be discounted to reflect the time value of money, uncertainty around the timing of cash flows and factors that market participants would reflect in pricing the future cash flows. IAS 36 also stipulates that the discount rate used to calculate the value in use shall be a pre-tax rate, although at the time of writing the IASB is considering amending this requirement.

In practice an external valuer is more likely to be engaged just to provide an estimate of the Fair Value less cost to sell, given that the calculation of value in use requires many inputs that are specific to the particular entity's business.

Chapter 6 IAS 40: Investment property

Investment property is defined in IAS 40 as property that is land or a building, or part of a building, or both, held by the owner to earn rentals or for capital appreciation, or both, rather than for:

a) use in the production or supply of goods or services or for administrative purposes, or

b) sale in the ordinary course of business.

This definition includes property that is being constructed or developed for future use as investment property. It includes property that is owned outright by the lessor and property held under a lease providing it is sublet or intended to be sublet under an operating lease or leases, see also IFRS 16 Leases.

Investment property is initially recognised in an entity's financial statements at its cost of purchase plus any directly attributable costs. For all subsequent statements the entity may adopt either the "Fair Value model" or the "cost model".

Fair value model

If the Fair Value model is adopted, the Fair Value of all investment property held as at the reporting date is measured in accordance with IFRS 13. The Fair Value therefore reflects the rental income from current leases and other assumptions market participants would use under current market conditions.

Where the Fair Value model is adopted, the depreciation provisions in IAS 16 outlined in Chapter 4 do not apply.

Cost Model

If the entity adopts the cost model it measures all its investment property in accordance with the cost model in IAS 16, unless it is classified as being held for sale, in which case IFRS 5 applies. However, even if an entity chooses the cost model to establish the carrying amount on the balance sheet, IAS 40 still requires the Fair Value at the reporting date to be disclosed in the notes to the financial statements.

In practice therefore, the current Fair Value of an investment property needs to be determined at every reporting date, regardless of which model is used. Most major holders of investment property that use IFRS adopt the Fair Value model, i.e. the Fair Value is incorporated in the balance sheet.

A limited exception to adopting the Fair Value model or disclosing Fair Value for all investment property held arises if, following acquisition of a property, exceptional circumstances mean that the Fair Value cannot be reliably estimated on a continuing basis. This may be because the market for comparable properties is likely to be inactive in the long term and there is insufficient data to estimate the value using a method such as discounted cash flow. In such cases an entity may adopt the cost model for that property. However, if an entity has previously measured the property at Fair Value it is required to continue to do so even if comparable transactions become less frequent or market prices become less readily available, thus preventing an entity opting out of revaluing property in periods when the market is weak.

Investment property under construction

Investment property under construction at the reporting date is effectively treated in the same way as completed property, i.e. the Fair Value model or the cost model may be adopted. If the Fair Value of an investment property under construction cannot be reliably measured, it can be measured at cost until either its Fair Value becomes reliably measurable or construction is completed, whichever is earlier. Investment property under construction can normally be valued using the "residual method" for which there are sophisticated models available that can automatically calculate the impact on value of a range of different scenarios for the time and cost required to complete and for the income expected on completion.

Chapter 7 IAS 41: Agriculture

IAS 41 applies to "Biological assets" and "agricultural produce" related to agricultural activity. It does not apply to:

- Bearer plants (see IAS 16)
- Land used or held for agricultural purposes (see IAS 16 or IAS 40)
- Intangible assets related to agricultural activity

A biological asset is a living animal or plant. Agricultural produce is the harvested produce of an entity's biological assets. The following are not bearer plants and therefore fall within the scope of IAS 41:

- plants cultivated to be harvested as agricultural produce (for example, trees grown for their timber);
- plants cultivated to produce agricultural produce when it is likely that the entity will also harvest and sell the plant as agricultural produce, e.g. trees that are cultivated both for their fruit and timber, other than incidental scrap sales.
- annual crops (for example, potatoes or wheat)

Biological assets and agricultural produce are recognised in the accounts of the entity that controls them at Fair Value less costs to sell. Fair value is generally determined in accordance with IFRS 13. The standard includes following provisions to clarify the application of Fair Value:

Biological assets or agricultural produce having similar attributes such as species, breed, age or quality may be grouped together for valuation purposes.

Contracts for sale for a fixed price at a future date are not necessarily relevant in establishing Fair Value which must reflect the price that would be agreed between market participants on the reporting date. No adjustment should be made to the Fair Value to reflect the existence of a contract for a future sale.

The Fair Value of the biological asset or agricultural produce does not take into account any financing cost, taxation or the costs of replacing or re-establishing the asset.

Biological assets are often physically attached to land, e.g. a plantation of trees. There may be no market for only the biological assets but an active market may exist for the combined assets, that is, the biological assets, the land and land improvements, as a package. Where this is the case, information regarding the combined assets can be used to measure the Fair Value of the biological assets. For example, the Fair Value of the land and land improvements may be deducted from the Fair Value of the combined assets to arrive at the Fair Value of biological assets.

Cost may sometimes be a good indicator of Fair Value, particularly when:

- little biological transformation has taken place since initial cost incurrence e.g. for seedlings planted immediately prior to the end of a reporting period or newly acquired livestock; or

- the impact of the biological transformation on price is not expected to be material e.g., the initial growth in a plantation that will not be harvested for many years.

If there are no quoted prices and any alternative Fair Value methods are clearly unreliable, at initial recognition an entity can measure a biological asset at cost less accumulated depreciation and impairment. However, once it becomes reliably measurable it must use the Fair Value less cost to sell.

Chapter 8 IFRS 3: Business combinations

The purpose of IFRS 3 is to set principles for the recognition and measurement of assets and liabilities acquired in a business combination, in other words in a takeover or merger. One of the parties to a business combination can always be identified as the acquirer, being the entity that obtains control of the other business. The formation of a joint venture or the acquisition of an asset or a group of assets that does not constitute a business are not business combinations.

The standard requires the acquiring entity to measure at Fair Value the identifiable assets acquired, and the liabilities assumed as at the date of acquisition. The difference between the Fair Value of all the identifiable assets, plus any interest held in the acquired business prior to the acquisition, is deemed to be goodwill. This can be a positive or negative figure.

An asset is identifiable if it either:

- is separable, i.e. capable of being separated or divided from the entity and sold, transferred, licensed, rented or exchanged regardless of whether the entity intends to do so; or

- arises from contractual or other legal rights, regardless of whether those rights are transferable or separable from the entity or from other rights and obligations.

There are exceptions to the recognition and

measurement requirements for some assets and liabilities such as contingent liabilities, income taxes, employee benefits, and assets held for sale. However, most tangible assets will be identifiable and therefore need to be measured at their Fair Value in accordance with IFRS 13 at the first reporting date following the combination. This is regardless of whether the acquired entity has previously carried those items at Fair Value or cost.

Valuations of property, plant and equipment acquired in a recent takeover or merger are becoming increasingly common as there are required even if the general policy of the acquiring entity is to carry such items at cost less depreciation under IAS 16.

Chapter 9 IFRS 5: Non-current assets held for sale and discontinued operations

A non-current asset is one for which full value will not be realised by an entity within one year. Examples include investments in other companies, intangible assets and tangible assets such as property, plant and equipment. To be classified as a "non-current asset held for sale" the asset must be available for immediate sale in its present condition and the sale must be highly probable within twelve months. This normally arises when a non-current asset is deemed surplus to an entity's continuing operations.

A non-current asset, or group of such assets, held for sale is measured at the lower of Fair Value less costs to sell and its carrying amount prior to its reclassification. To comply with the requirement for a sale to be highly probable there needs to be commitment by the entity's management to the sale, and to active marketing of the asset at a reasonable price.

Fair value is measured in accordance with IFRS 13, and the valuer may additionally be asked to advise on the probable costs to sell.

Chapter 10   IFRS 16: Leases

This standard was issued by the IASB in 2016, and replaced the earlier standard for lease accounting, IAS17, from 1 January 2019. It significantly changed the way in which lessees have to account for leases, although the regime for lessors remains similar to that under IAS 17. The standard applies to all leases, including subleases, except for:

- leases to explore for or use minerals, oil, natural gas and similar non-regenerative resources;
- leases of biological assets held by a lessee;
- service concession arrangements;
- licences of intellectual property granted by a lessor and
- rights held by a lessee under licensing agreements for items such as films, videos, plays, manuscripts, patents and copyrights within the scope of IAS 38 Intangible Assets.

Lessees

Under the previous regime lessees had to determine whether a lease was an "operating lease" or a "finance lease". If it was classed as an operating lease, the rental payments were accounted for as an operating expense on the profit and loss account, but no other aspects of the lease needed to be included in the financial statements. Critics argued that this meant that future lease liabilities did not need to be disclosed, which could give a misleading view of an entity's overall financial position.

Under IFRS 16 a lessee has to account for both the "right of use asset" and the corresponding liability on its balance sheet. At the commencement of a lease, the asset is measured at "cost", which is deemed to be the present value of the liability, plus any payment made at or before entering into the lease, any direct costs incurred entering into the lease and the estimated cost of any restoration required by the lease at the end of the term. Variable lease payments based on an index or a rate are included in the initial measurement of the lease liability and are initially measured using the index or rate as at the commencement date.

The discount rate to be used in determining the present value of the liability is the "discount rate implicit in the lease", which is the rate that causes the present value of the lease payments and the residual value of the asset at the end of the lease to equal the Fair Value of the asset and any direct initial costs of the lessor. If this discount rate cannot be easily determined, then the lessee can use its "incremental borrowing rate".

After a lease has commenced a lessee uses the same "cost model" as described above to measure the asset and liability, except:
- If the right of use asset is an investment property and a lessee applies the Fair Value

model in IAS 40 the lessee shall also apply that Fair Value model to that asset, or

- If the right of use asset is a class of property, plant and equipment to which the lessee applies the revaluation model in IAS 16, a lessee may apply that revaluation model.

It can be seen that although the measurement of the right of use asset is referred to in the standard as a cost, calculating this cost requires the application of a number of valuation techniques, for example to determine the Fair Value of the asset, the residual value at the end of the lease and the discount rate implicit in the lease. At the time or writing the extent to which valuers may be called upon to assist entities in determining their lease assets and liabilities remains to be seen.

In most cases, any investment property held by a lessee investor under a head lease, will be accounted for using the Fair Value model under IAS 40. This is effectively how this type of interest has been treated for many years and should not give rise to any different valuation challenges. However, challenges can be anticipated for entities in applying the new standard to operational property. Previously, most occupational leases were classified as "operating leases" and therefore there was no need to value the asset or liability. For entities with large numbers of leasehold properties questions will arise over how the principles in IFRS 16 apply to properties that are not standalone buildings, e.g. units within a shopping mall or floors within an office tower, where some rights are exclusive and others shared. A practical consensus will probably emerge between preparers, users and auditors as to how the new provisions should be applied but until that time significant debate can be expected.

Lessors

For lessors, the requirements of IFRS 16 are very similar to those in IAS 17. There is a requirement for an entity to classify each of its leases to another entity as either a finance lease or an operating lease.

A finance lease transfers substantially all the risks and rewards incidental to ownership of an underlying asset. An operating lease does not transfer substantially all the risks and rewards incidental to ownership of an underlying asset.

Property which is held under a lease and then leased, or intended to be leased, to others under one or more operating leases is classed as investment property and therefore accounted for under IAS 40. However, if the lease is a finance lease then it will not meet the criteria for investment property under IAS 40 and needs to be accounted for under IFRS 16.

Whether an agreement is a finance lease depends on the substance rather than the form of the contract. IFRS 16 provides the following examples of situations that could be indicative of a finance lease, either individually or in combination:

- the lease transfers ownership of the asset to the lessee at or before the end of the lease term,
- the lessee has the option to purchase the asset at a discounted price,
- the lease term is for the major part of the economic life of the asset,
- the present value of the minimum lease payments at the inception of the lease amounts substantially all of the Fair Value of the leased asset,
- the leased assets are of such a specialised nature that only the lessee can use them without major modification,
- if the lessee can cancel the lease, the lessor's losses associated with the cancellation are borne by the lessee,
- gains or losses from the fluctuation in the Fair Value of the residual accrue to the lessee,
- the lessee has the ability to continue the lease for a secondary period at a rent that is substantially lower than the market rent.

It is emphasised that these are just examples that may indicate a finance lease and should not be regarded as conclusive. If it is clear from other features that the lease does not transfer substantially all risks and rewards incidental to ownership, the lease is classified as an operating lease. For example, this may be the case if ownership of the asset transfers at the end of the lease for a variable payment equal to its then value, or if there are regular reviews of the rent, to the then market level or by reference to an inflation index.

Finance leases are common for plant and equipment where they are offered as an alternative means of funding the acquisition of capital equipment. Indeed, there is an apocryphal story that a former Chairman of the IASB declared it was his ambition to fly on an aircraft that was actually on the balance sheet of the airline before he retired.

In contrast, finance leases of land and buildings are less common. They will generally arise where the lease is clearly created as a way of funding the eventual purchase of the property by the lessee, e.g. by means of an option to acquire the lessor's interest for a nominal sum after the specified rental payments have been made. Occasionally, leases that are not clearly structured as finance agreements may meet some of the criteria of a finance lease, e.g. where the rental payments do not reflect the underlying value of the property. In such cases, a more detailed analysis of the value of the risks and benefits transferred from lessor to lessee may be required in order to determine the correct classification.

Valuers may well find themselves being asked to provide valuation advice to assist lessors in determining whether a lease of land or buildings is correctly classified as an operating lease or finance lease, This could include providing opinions as to the economic life of the asset at the commencement of the lease, the value of the underlying asset and the extent to which the risks and rewards of ownership are transferred by the lease.

A further complication is that IFRS 16 requires that the land and building elements of a lease be considered separately for the purposes of classification. If it appears that the element of the lease attributable to the building could be a finance lease, it will be necessary to make an allocation of the initial rent based on the relative Fair Values of the interest in each element at the inception of the lease.

Where the land and building elements are clearly identifiable, this allocation of the rent can usually be undertaken reliably. An example would be a lease of land with a specialised building which is of use only to the present lessee and which would be at the end of its economic life at the expiry of the lease term. The land element would be normally expected to be an operating lease as it would be of value to the lessor at the end of the term, whereas the building element would be a finance lease.

Where a reliable allocation between land and buildings cannot be made, the standard requires that whole lease should be treated as a finance lease. In this context it should be noted that if it were clear both elements were operating leases, the allocation exercise would not be necessary, as it would be classified as an investment property. For a lease of land and buildings in which the amount for the land element is immaterial to the lease, a lessor may treat the land and buildings as a single unit for the purpose of lease classification.

Lease classification is made at the inception of the lease. Classification involves an assessment of the degree to which economic benefits are transferred by a lease. In many cases a qualitative assessment of the lease terms will quickly indicate the correct classification without the need for a quantitative analysis. However, valuations may be required to help establish benefits accruing to the lessor and lessee respectively, e.g. in estimating the residual value at the end of the lease to establish if the lease is for a major part of the asset's economic life.

Chapter 11 Professional Requirements

This briefing is produced for valuation professionals generally, not for members of any particular professional body. However, many professionals will be subject to professional requirements and standards relating to the undertaking and reporting of valuations that are intended for use in a published financial statement.

These professional requirements could relate to the credentials or experience necessary to undertake valuations for financial reporting, rules aimed at ensuring the appropriate independence of the valuer or to specific disclosures or conditions required in the report.

By way of example, the RICS Valuation – Global Standards 2017 (the "Red Book") requires certain disclosures aimed at demonstrating that the valuer has the required degree of objectivity and independence from the reporting entity whenever the valuation is likely to relied on by a third party, including valuations appearing in financial statements. These disclosures, which must be included in the terms of engagement, the report and any published reference to the report, are as follows:

- PS2.5.3 requires a member or member firm to disclose any case within the last twelve months where they acted for the reporting entity in either negotiating the acquisition of an asset or received an introductory fee. This is mainly applicable to property companies and funds who retain a firm to undertake regular revaluations of their portfolio but may also use that firm to advise on new acquisitions. The purpose of this disclosure is to provide transparency to third parties about the relationship between the valuer and the reporting entity.

- PS2.5.4 requires firms to have a policy of rotating the lead valuer responsible for recurring revaluations of the same asset or portfolio, recommending that this be done at least once every seven years.

- PS2.5.5 requires that policy to be disclosed in all instructions that involve recurring valuations at specified intervals, together with how long the same valuer has been responsible for the valuation as lead signatory. The purpose of these requirements is to avoid the threat to objectivity that can result from over familiarity with a particular asset or portfolio.

- PS2.5.7 requires firms to disclose if the total fees earned from the reporting entity in the preceding twelve months represent a "minimal", "substantial" or "significant" proportion of its total fee income. Minimal is below 5%, significant between 5% and 25% and significant above 25%.

RICS national standards can amend or extend its global standards, and therefore any RICS, member undertaking a valuation for inclusion in a financial statement needs to be aware of any variation of the above disclosures where country specific standards are applied. Members of other professional organisations may also have specific professional standards or codes that apply to financial reporting valuations.

Illustrative Examples

Before reading these Illustrative Examples, it is important to remember that the preparation of a valuation for inclusion in a financial statement does not require the use of techniques or methods that are any different from those used in valuation for other purposes. The market (sales comparison), income and depreciated replacement cost approaches can all be used, and the criteria for their use is identical to those that determine which approach should be used for any other purpose. The principal differences between valuations that are intended for use in a Financial Statement and other types of valuation are the specific reporting requirements and, in particular, the need to identify and disclose appropriate assumptions. The examples therefore mainly focus on the presentation of the valuation, rather than its calculation.

IE 1   An owner occupied property with a limited market.

A very large owner-occupied office on the outskirts of a regional city is fully utilised by the reporting entity for its operations. However, if the entity were to vacate there would be little or no demand from other owner-occupiers due to the property's size and location. If it were to become surplus to the entity's requirements, the building probably would be demolished and the land used for another purpose. How should such a property be valued for inclusion in the occupying entity's accounts?

As this property is owned and occupied for operational

purposes, the relevant standard is IAS 16 Property, Plant and Equipment. Under the revaluation option, the Fair Value has to be determined in accordance with IFRS 13 *Fair Value Measurements*. IAS 1 *Presentation of Financial Statements* provides the overriding criteria for the presentation of financial statements under IFRS and is also relevant to this example.

One of the overriding requirements of IAS 1 is that management shall make an assessment of the entity's ability to continue as a going concern, and that the financial statements shall be prepared on a going concern basis unless management either intends to liquidate the entity or cease trading, or has no realistic alternative but to do so. The reporting entity is therefore not only in existence at the reporting date but will normally be deemed to continuing its operations.

This going concern presumption means that while Fair Value reflects the price that would be agreed between market participants and ignores the particular circumstances of the reporting entity, it does not follow that the existence of the entity has to be ignored. There is at least one market participant who requires the property for operational purposes, albeit that hypothetical entity is not the reporting entity. Further, although IFRS 13 describes Fair Value as an exit price, this does not mean that a scenario has to be envisaged under which the reporting entity would actually dispose of the property providing it had a continuing need for it in the business.

The question being asked of the valuer is therefore "*what*

would be the price that a seller of this property would agree with a buyer requiring it for its continuing business operations?" rather than "what would the entity expect to receive for this property if it no longer required it?" In cases where there is an active market for the asset there would be little discernible difference between the answers to either of these questions, but in this example the difference between assuming at least one willing buyer requiring the property for the use for which it was designed and the probability that there are none at all becomes significant.

Further indicators of the correct approach can be found in IFRS 13. Paragraph 21 states that even when there is no observable market, the assumed transaction should be considered from the perspective of the entity that holds the asset. Paragraphs 22 and 23 describe the assumptions to be made about the market participants referenced in the Fair Value definition. Firstly, the market participants are to be deemed to be acting in their economic best interest. Secondly, a specific market participant does not need to be identified, but that the characteristics of market participants that would enter into such a transaction have to be considered. This means that the buyer will not over pay, but equally that the seller will be aware of unique facility offered by the property and the costs that would be incurred by the buyer if it were not available and negotiate accordingly.

The similarities between IVSC Market Value and IFRS Fair Value were discussed in Chapter 2, and correct application of either should produce the same result. No difference arises from the need to consider the transaction from the perspective of the present holder where there is no discernible market in IFRS. The conceptual framework for Market Value clearly states that the present owner of an asset is included among the cohort of "willing buyers" that constitute the market. Consequently, it would be just as wrong to ignore the demand for the property from the current owner under Market Value, unless they have expressly excluded themselves from the market, for example by declaring the property surplus to requirements.

There can be no specific method or technique that will provide the valuer with the difference in value for a unique property for which there is only one prospective buyer and one for which there are none. Rather the valuer needs to replicate the thought processes of the hypothetical parties. The seller has something unique that the buyer requires, but the buyer may have alternative ways of meeting that requirement. The buyer's alternatives could include dispersing the operations among a number of smaller buildings or buying land and constructing their own building. These alternatives will have costs but may also have advantages which would influence the buyer in deciding the maximum they would pay for the subject property. On the other hand, the seller may have realistic prospects for an alternative use or redevelopment of the property which would influence the minimum amount they would accept.

Only after thorough research and consideration of the facts of the specific situation can the valuer reach a valid conclusion as to the result of this hypothetical negotiation, but it would lie between the extremes of the cost to the buyer of creating an alternative facility on the one hand and the amount the seller would receive if there was no buyer that required the existing facility provided by the property.

Having determined what the Fair Value should be, it is probable that the valuer may have also concluded that if the property were to become surplus to the current owner's operational requirements, a significantly lower figure could be realised. When reporting the value for inclusion in the financial statements it would also be prudent to indicate this, and, if appropriate, to also provide the "if surplus" value, so that management is aware of the effect that a future change in their operational requirements may have on the appropriate carrying amount on the balance sheet.

IE2   Calculating the depreciable amount of a building

An entity owns a modern industrial building which houses specialist equipment for a process which the entity estimates has a useful life of no more than five years due to technological advances. After that time the building will be surplus to the entity's requirements. The valuer estimates that the building has an economic life of twenty years but has to estimate its value assuming it is at the end of its useful life to the entity, when it will still have fifteen years of economic life remaining.

The approach is to first establish the value of the land element, which cannot be subject to depreciation under IAS16. This is then deducted from the Carrying Amount. Note that although in most cases the valuer will be asked to make the apportionment of the current Fair Value of the entity's interest in the land and buildings combined, the entity is required to calculate the depreciable amount regardless of whether it adopts the cost model or revaluation model. The Carrying Amount can therefore be the historic cost less any accumulated depreciation instead of the current Fair Value.

Carrying Amount of building and land:	10,000,000
Value of land without building ignoring any higher value for alternative use.	3,000,000
Notional Value of building.	7,000,000

In a simple example where the economic life of the building to the entity is indefinite, i.e. it is no different from the expected economic life of the building to the market as a whole the Depreciable Amount would be 7,000,000 and the Residual Amount 3,000,000. The entity would have to depreciate the 7,000,000 on a systematic basis over the whole of the anticipated life of the building. However, in this example the economic life to the entity is significantly shorter, which requires a further stage of calculation by the valuer.

The valuer has to imagine that the building is five years older and in the condition expected at the end of its useful life to the entity. Since in this example the building is estimated to still have a significant useful economic life at this date it is reasonable to assume that it will be in the current owner's interest to maintain it in reasonable repair to maximise the chance of selling, therefore it is not appropriate in this example to assume a significant deterioration in condition. However, it can be observed in the market that older buildings are not as valuable as newer ones. On the basis of comparison of the sale prices achieved for buildings which are five years older than the subject the valuer concludes that the value at the end of its useful life to the entity would be 6,000,000.

The Residual Value is therefore the value of the land plus the value of the building that will be remaining at the end of the useful life, i.e. 3,000,000 + 6,000,000 = 9,000,000.

The Depreciable Amount is the difference between the Carrying Amount and the Residual Value, i.e. 1,000,000. The entity then has to depreciate this amount by making a charge against income over the each of the next five years which reflects the pattern by which the benefit of the building is used up over that period.

About the Author

This Briefing has been written by Chris Thorne FRICS. Chris's career includes over 35 years as a commercial property valuer in private practice, starting with a small regional firm in the UK in the 1970s, and culminating as technical head of valuation for an international property services firm. Between 2010 and 2015 he was Technical Director of the International Valuation Standards Council.

Chris was also active as a volunteer member of various RICS boards and committees between 1993 and 2010, including eight years as chairman of the Red Book Editorial Board and a number of years as chairman of the Valuation for Financial Statements Group. Between 2008 and 2010 he was also chairman of the International Valuation Standards Board, a position he had to relinquish when appointed Technical Director.

Between 2007 and 2010 he was a member of the FASB Valuation Resource Group in the USA which advised the Board on issues raised by users of the US accounting standards following the introduction of its Fair Value standard FAS 157 (now renamed Topic 820). He also made presentations on valuation to the IASB to assist its deliberations during the development of IFRS 13.

In these various professional and voluntary roles, Chris had considerable experience working with accounting standard setters to reconcile valuation concepts and terminology with the accounting objectives and to ensure that valuation professionals understood the appropriate valuation approaches and assumptions.

In 2015 he cofounded Valuology Ltd, which provides advice to valuation firms, valuation users and governmental organisations on risk management and best practice in the field of valuation.

www.ingramcontent.com/pod-product-compliance
Lightning Source LLC
Chambersburg PA
CBHW070501220526
45466CB00004B/1914